THE VACCINE

A TALE OF SPIES AND ALIENS

by LINKED IN AND TOWN HALL ACHIEVER OF THE YEAR
EY NOMINEE ENTREPRENEUR OF THE YEAR
GRAND HOMAGE LYS DIVERSITY
WORLD TOP100 DOCTORS

Dr. BAK NGUYEN, DMD

&

WILLIAM BAK

TO EVERYONE LOOKING TO UNDERSTAND A VACCINE
FROM A SCIENCE STANDPOINT, PUT INTO WORDS
YOU'LL UNDERSTAND.

by Dr. BAK NGUYEN
& WILLIAM BAK

Published by: DR. BAK PUBLISHING COMPANY
Scientifically revised by Dr. JEAN DE SERRES
Reviewed by BRENDA GARCIA

ABOUT THE AUTHORS

From Canada, **Dr. BAK NGUYEN**, Nominee Ernst and Young Entrepreneur of the year, Grand Homage Lys DIVERSITY, LinkedIn & TownHall Achiever of the year and TOP 100 Doctors 2021. Dr Bak is a cosmetic dentist, CEO and founder of Mdex & Co. His company is revolutionizing the dental field. Speaker and motivator, he wrote 72 books over 36 months accumulating many world records (to be officialized). His books are covering:

- **ENTREPRENEURSHIP**
- **LEADERSHIP**
- **QUEST OF IDENTITY**
- **DENTISTRY AND MEDICINE**
- **PARENTING**
- **CHILDREN BOOKS**
- **PHILOSOPHY**

In 2003, he founded Mdex, a dental company upon which in 2018, he launched the most ambitious private endeavour to reform the dental industry, Canada wide. Philosopher, he has close to his heart the quest of happiness of the people surrounding him, patients and colleagues alike. In 2020, he launched an International collaborative initiative named **THE ALPHAS** to share knowledge and for Entrepreneurs and Doctors to thrive through the Greatest Pandemic and Economic depression of our time.

In 2016, he co-found with Tranie Vo, Emotive World Incorporated, a tech research company to use technology to empower happiness and sharing. U.A.X. the ultimate audio experience is the landmark project on which the team is advancing, utilizing the technics of the movie industry and the advancement in ARTIFICIAL INTELLIGENCE to save the book industry and to upgrade the continuing education space.

These projects have allowed Dr Nguyen to attract interests from the international and diplomatic community and he is now the center of a global discussion in the wellbeing and the future of the health profession. It is in that matter that he shares his thoughts and encourages the health community to share their own stories.

"It's not worth it go through it alone! Together, we stand, alone, we fall."

Motivational speaker and serial entrepreneur, philosopher and author, from his own words, Dr Nguyen describes himself as a dentist by circumstances, an entrepreneur by nature and a communicator by passion.

He also holds recognitions from the Canadian Parliament and the Canadian Senate.

From Canada, **William Bak**, is a 10 years old prodigy. At the age of 8 years old, he co-wrote a series of chicken books with his dad, Dr. Bak. Together, they are changing the world, one mind at a time, writing books for kids. So far, they have 23 books together.

He co-wrote the 10 chicken books in ENGLISH and then, had to translate his own books in FRENCH. This is how he has 20 chicken books. William also co-wrote 2 parenting books with his dad, Dr. Bak, THE BOOK OF LEGENDS volumes 1 and 2. Volume 3 is in production.

To promote his books, William embraced the stage for the first time in 2019 talking to a crowd of 300+ people. Since, he has appeared in many videos to talk about his books and upcoming projects.

In the midst of COVID, he got bored and started his YOUTUBE CHANNEL : GAMEBAK, reviewing video games.
By the end of 2020, he has joined THE ALPHAS as the youngest anchor of the upcoming world project COVIDCONOMICS in which he will give his perspective and host the opinions of his generation.

"I will show you. I won't force you. But I won't wait for you.
- William Bak and Dr. Bak

Writing with his Dad, William holds world records to be officialized:

- The youngest author writing in 2 languages
- Co-author of 8 books within a month
- The first kid to have written 20 children books

THE VACCINE

BY DR. BAK NGUYEN & WILLIAM BAK

PROLOGUE

QUESTION #1
WHAT IS A VACCINE?

QUESTION #2
WHY DOES THE VIRUS WANT TO GET
INTO OUR BODY?

QUESTION #3
WHERE DO YOU GET THE VIRUS?

QUESTION #4
WHAT IS THE VIRUS DOING ONCE
INSIDE OUR BODY?

QUESTION #5
WHY SHOULD WE GET VACCINATED?

QUESTION #6
IS IT DANGEROUS?

QUESTION #7
HOW DOES IT WORK?

QUESTION #8
IS IT WITH THE VIRUS THAT WE ARE
INJECTING OURSELVES WITH?

QUESTION #9
CAN WE DIE FROM THAT?

QUESTION #10
IT DOES NOT MAKE SENSE TO INJECT
OURSELVES WITH THE VIRUS, SO WHY
DO IT?

QUESTION #11
CAN I EAT THE VACCINE INSTEAD OF
HAVING AN INJECTION?

QUESTION #12
IS THAT ALL TRUE PAPA? OR YOU ARE
JUST PLAYING GAMES WITH ME?

PROLOGUE
THE QUESTIONS

BY DR. BAK NGUYEN & WILLIAM BAK

T his morning,
William, my 10-year-old son
Woke me up with a big question mark
on his forehead.

Papa, what is a vaccine?
And why should we have one?
Is it dangerous?
How does it work?

Is it the Coronavirus
That we are injecting ourselves with?
Can we die from it?

Papa, it doesn't make sense
To inject the Coronavirus in us, so why do it?

I don't know where that all came from,
But these were surely legitimate questions.

William, I know you have many questions.
Let's address them one by one,
Shall we?

> "There are no stupid questions. Just stupid answers."
> - Dr. Bak Nguyen

If you could just let me
Brush my teeth first...

QUESTION #1

WHAT IS A VACCINE?

BY DR. BAK NGUYEN & WILLIAM BAK

A vaccine is a solution
That medical professionals will inject
Into people to prevent them
From becoming sick.

It is an inactive piece of the virus
Called RNA that is injected into your body
So your body can form **antibodies**
To fight the real virus.

"Hein???"

– William Bak

You see William,
A virus is like an alien invasion,
When the aliens are coming in.
Our body needs their police forces
And army to stop them.

Most of the time,
The Aliens are obvious
And easy to recognize.

Some other times,

They are invisible to us

Or are in disguise,

Looking like the local population.

Then, like spies,

They infiltrate our bodies

And prepare their invasion.

So a vaccine is a way for our police forces

And army to identify and to target

The alien spies in disguise.

This is what a vaccine is,

From a science standpoint

Put into words you'll understand.

QUESTION #2

WHY DOES THE VIRUS WANT TO GET INTO OUR BODY?

BY DR. BAK NGUYEN & WILLIAM BAK

The answer to this one is simple.
They are looking for a warm home.

Virus are much smaller than human
We are like a planet to them
They look at us and see a planet
One to explore
One to conquer

Our body is home to our cells
Cells are our population
Viruses are even smaller than cells,
Like any good alien invaders
They are getting inside of our cells
And taking over.

This is why, from the outside
Our cells cannot make the difference
Between a normal cell
And a contaminated one.

Once a cell gets contaminated
It becomes sick
And slowly will morph into a zombie
By then, they are easy to identify
But then, it might be too late.

This is why we need to deliver

The special package before the invasion

So our body has the time to train

And to create special units

Code named **ANTIBODIES**.

This is what a vaccine is,

From a science standpoint

Put into words you'll understand.

WHERE DO YOU
GET THE VIRUS?

BY DR. BAK NGUYEN & WILLIAM BAK

Y ou can get the virus
From any entrances of your body
From your mouth, from your nose
From your eyes, from your ears
And even from your skin.

The virus is so small
That it can get in
From all of these places.

Your safe bet is to clean
Your hands often
And to wear a special mask
So you block the entrances.

Until you have a vaccine
And have a way to stop
The virus from getting inside of your body.

This is what a vaccine is,
From a science standpoint
Put into words you'll understand.

QUESTION #4

WHAT IS THE VIRUS DOING ONCE INSIDE OUR BODY?

BY DR. BAK NGUYEN & WILLIAM BAK

Once inside of our body
The first virus will try
To establish a base.

They will infiltrate some of our cells
And regroup.
The viruses have no means of communication
So they cannot call for reinforcement

They are the invasion!
Now that they are in,
They stay discreet as spies
And identify what cells
To take over.

Then, once inside the cell
The virus will copy itself
To create his own squads of spies

If no one has arrested them yet
The spies will get out
And find new cells to infect
Each time, they find a cell,
They make a new base,
A new factory to make
More aliens like them.

If our police forces act on time
They surround the contaminated cells
Before they become zombies
And put them away.

If we act too late
Most of our cells will already be contaminated
And be either sick or zombies
By then, it might be too late
And the police forces will have to call the army

Once the army arrive
It is no joke.
They will torch all the cells of the neighborhood
If that does not work,
They will be calling for a nuke

You do not want a nuke attack
Inside of your body.
This is only, if they get ran over by
The Zombies cells and the aliens inside.

This is what a vaccine is,
From a science standpoint
Put into words you'll understand.

QUESTION #5

WHY SHOULD WE GET VACCINATED?

BY DR. BAK NGUYEN & WILLIAM BAK

A vaccine is a special package
For your body
To form **ANTIBODIES**
To fight the virus.

"Hein???"

– William Bak

It is a way for your army
To have special goggles
To see the alien spies
And to stop them.

Knowing who they are,
They won't be torching the entire neighborhood,
But could now single out
Only the alien spies.

Would you refuse such tools
For your police forces?

If you refuse,

They will end up with nothing

To single out the alien spies

From the rest of your normal population of cells,

Either they will arrest

The wrong people, innocent people

Or they will fail at their task

Of protecting your body

And the alien spies will take over!

That's your choice!

This is what a vaccine is,

From a science standpoint

Put into words you'll understand.

QUESTION #6
IS IT DANGEROUS?

BY DR. BAK NGUYEN & WILLIAM BAK

V accines have been around for centuries
And have saved millions of people
From infections.

You surely have received many vaccines
For the different viruses yourself.
You are strong and healthy, no?

In rare cases,
Some people develop adverse side effects
And there are complications.
But that is the exception,
Not the general rule.

Otherwise, we would all be dead by now
Since we have all been vaccinated.

"So, is it dangerous???"
– William Bak

When your soldiers
Receive the special equipment,

They must learn to use it
And to adapt their ways.

Since those are goggles
And special ammo,
Sometimes special bombs,
Some of your soldiers may get hurt
Learning how to use them.

Vaccines are weapons to fight aliens (virus),
They are not toys.
They are efficient.
Done respecting the safety protocol,
They are of good use
And will do much good.
Otherwise, they may cause harm.

In the case of the people
Getting sick from a vaccine,
It is not their fault,
We just need to find a way
So their body can understand
The safety protocol of the vaccine.

Not all bodies are talking the same tongue.

This is what a vaccine is,

From a science standpoint

Put into words you'll understand.

HOW DOES IT WORK?

BY DR. BAK NGUYEN & WILLIAM BAK

Well, a vaccine is
An inactive part of a virus
Called RNA.

Those will be injected
Into our bodies
And be copied to form
Detectors of that specific virus.
We call them, The **ANTIBODIES**.

"So they are the enemies of our
bodies?"

- William Bak

No, there are the detectors
Identifying the enemies
And the alien spies.

The Antibodies are special units
Patrolling our body to arrest the virus.
If they identify one,
They attach themselves to it

43

And call for reinforcements.

Then, the police force will arrest
The alien spy (virus)
And put it away.

The special units
Are called **ANTIBODIES**.
The police forces and the army
Are called **WHITE CELLS**.

If the police arrests the alien spies,
They stop the invasion
And the war never happens.
This is when you do not get sick.
Otherwise, you might need bedtime
And hot noodle chicken soup.

This is what a vaccine is,
From a science standpoint
Put into words you'll understand.

IS IT WITH THE VIRUS THAT WE ARE INJECTING OURSELVES WITH?

BY DR. BAK NGUYEN & WILLIAM BAK

As I said earlier,
We are injecting
Only a little piece of the virus,
Not the virus itself.

It's like having now
A heat signature of the alien spies
And a photography of their faces,

It does not mean
That we have opened the door
Or have granted them access
With a passport of any kind.

Only now, we know how they look like.
And our special forces might identify them
So our police forces
Can arrest them, the alien spies.

This is what a vaccine is,
From a science standpoint
Put into words you'll understand.

CAN WE DIE FROM THAT?

BY DR. BAK NGUYEN & WILLIAM BAK

T he answer is
There are risks of complications.

Some bodies won't be able to read
The safety protocol
And might react to the vaccine
As if it was the alien spy itself.

In that case,
Instead of creating a special unit
That will duplicate the photos
And the heat signature,
They will call in the army
And nuke the vaccine instead.

In a nuke, called **inflammation**
There is no distinction between
The aliens or the normal cell population
Everyone gets hurt.

The harm is the nuke
That they launched themselves
On the vaccine.

Rest assured,
There is no risk o,

But that does not
Happen often.

But it still happens sometimes.
This is why it is so important
That the safety protocols
Are delivered
And understood by
All our bodies

A vaccine is not the enemy
It is a way to create
Special units that will
Identify the alien spies
So our body won't nuke
Itself by mistake

"When is it too late for a vaccine?"
- William Bak

A vaccine will only work
Before the virus get inside of your body

Or when very few spies are present

But once the zombie cells have appeared
It is too late for the vaccine
By then, you will have to call the army
And to nuke a few neighborhoods of cells.

It is then that you will feel sick
That you will have a fever
And hopefully, after a few days
You will get better.

Your army will have wiped out the invasion

This is what a vaccine is,
From a science standpoint
Put into words you'll understand.

IT DOES NOT MAKE SENSE TO INJECT OURSELVES WITH THE VIRUS, SO WHY DO IT?

BY DR. BAK NGUYEN & WILLIAM BAK

Well, you are right.
It does not make sense to inject
Ourselves with the Coronavirus.
A vaccine is not that.

Once more,
We are sending a special package
To our body so it can prepare itself
For the invasion

From the special package
They have the instruction and weapon
To train special units that will
Identify the alien spies specifically.

We are not sending alien spies
Into our body,
Just ways to identify them
And to prepare our troops,
The special units (**antibodies**)

This is what a vaccine is,
From a science standpoint
Put into words you'll understand.

CAN I EAT THE VACCINE INSTEAD OF HAVING AN INJECTION?

BY DR. BAK NGUYEN & WILLIAM BAK

U nfortunately, the vaccine
Need to be injected
Inside of your body
To be efficient.

If you put it in your mouth,
By eating it
Or drinking it
It won't work.

"Why Papa, it is still going inside your
body..."
— William Bak

Think of it this way,
You need to deliver
The special package
To the special unit's headquarters
Instead, if you eat it,
You are delivering it to the kitchen
How do you think that it will work?

After the kitchen, the toilet is next.

If you eat or drink the vaccine

Your special troops keep waiting

And never receive your envoy

"Really papa, the kitchen?"

- William Bak

Actually, it is your stomach

And the toilet is your intestine

It was just easier

To picture them that way.

In reality, once in your stomach

The vaccine will be digested

And decomposed like food

And the package will be terminated.

In that case, the aliens

Will be victorious.

Would you want that?

So do not eat nor drink

The vaccine!

This is what a vaccine is,

From a science standpoint

Put into words you'll understand.

IS THAT ALL TRUE PAPA? OR YOU ARE JUST PLAYING GAMES WITH ME?

BY DR. BAK NGUYEN & WILLIAM BAK

This is all the truth.
I learned that becoming a doctor.
Even a dentist has to know
How a vaccine works.

I just put the explanations into
Words that you would understand easily,
Talking about special units,
Aliens spies, and invasion.

Actually, I am not that far from reality.
In med school,
We talked about virus infections
As invasions and we often compared
Our body and its defence reactions
As war measures.

Ask all doctors,
They will tell you their version of this story,
And the theme of war will always surface.
Why? Because it is what really happens
Inside our body,
A fight and a war to keep
The virus at bay.

And with this,

Most of his question marks were gone.

Now a new one appears on his face.

"Papa, are you hungry?"

- William Bak

This is what a vaccine is,

From a science standpoint

Put into words you'll understand.

ABOUT THE AUTHORS

From Canada, **Dr. BAK NGUYEN**, Nominee Ernst and Young Entrepreneur of the year, Grand Homage Lys DIVERSITY, LinkedIn & TownHall Achiever of the year and TOP 100 Doctors 2021. Dr Bak is a cosmetic dentist, CEO and founder of Mdex & Co. His company is revolutionizing the dental field. Speaker and motivator, he wrote 72 books over 36 months accumulating many world records (to be officialized). His books are covering:

- **ENTREPRENEURSHIP**
- **LEADERSHIP**
- **QUEST OF IDENTITY**
- **DENTISTRY AND MEDICINE**
- **PARENTING**
- **CHILDREN BOOKS**
- **PHILOSOPHY**

In 2003, he founded Mdex, a dental company upon which in 2018, he launched the most ambitious private endeavour to reform the dental industry, Canada wide. Philosopher, he has close to his heart the quest of happiness of the people surrounding him, patients and colleagues alike. In 2020, he launched an International collaborative initiative named **THE ALPHAS** to share knowledge and for Entrepreneurs and Doctors to thrive through the Greatest Pandemic and Economic depression of our time.

In 2016, he co-found with Tranie Vo, Emotive World Incorporated, a tech research company to use technology to empower happiness and sharing. U.A.X. the ultimate audio experience is the landmark project on which the team is advancing, utilizing the technics of the movie industry and the advancement in ARTIFICIAL INTELLIGENCE to save the book industry and to upgrade the continuing education space.

These projects have allowed Dr Nguyen to attract interests from the international and diplomatic community and he is now the center of a global discussion in the wellbeing and the future of the health profession. It is in that matter that he shares his thoughts and encourages the health community to share their own stories.

"It's not worth it go through it alone! Together, we stand, alone, we fall."

Motivational speaker and serial entrepreneur, philosopher and author, from his own words, Dr Nguyen describes himself as a dentist by circumstances, an entrepreneur by nature and a communicator by passion.

He also holds recognitions from the Canadian Parliament and the Canadian Senate.

www.DrBakNguyen.com

From Canada, **William Bak**, is a 10 years old prodigy. At the age of 8 years old, he co-wrote a series of chicken books with his dad, Dr. Bak. Together, they are changing the world, one mind at a time, writing books for kids. So far, they have 23 books together.

He co-wrote the 10 chicken books in ENGLISH and then, had to translate his own books in FRENCH. This is how he has 20 chicken books. William also co-wrote 2 parenting books with his dad, Dr. Bak, THE BOOK OF LEGENDS volumes 1 and 2. Volume 3 is in production.

To promote his books, William embraced the stage for the first time in 2019 talking to a crowd of 300+ people. Since, he has appeared in many videos to talk about his books and upcoming projects.

In the midst of COVID, he got bored and started his YOUTUBE CHANNEL : GAMEBAK, reviewing video games.
By the end of 2020, he has joined THE ALPHAS as the youngest anchor of the upcoming world project COVIDCONOMICS in which he will give his perspective and host the opinions of his generation.

"I will show you. I won't force you. But I won't wait for you.
- William Bak and Dr. Bak

Writing with his Dad, William holds world records to be officialized:

- The youngest author writing in 2 languages
- Co-author of 8 books within a month
- The first kid to have written 20 children books

UAX

ULTIMATE AUDIO EXPERIENCE

A new way to learn and enjoy Audiobooks. Made to be entertaining while keeping the self-educational value of a book, UAX will appeal to both auditive and visual people. UAX is the blockbuster of the Audiobooks.

UAX will cover most of Dr Bak's books, and is now negotiating to bring more authors and more titles to the UAX concept. Now streaming on Spotify, Apple Music and available for download on all major music platforms. Give it a try today!

AMAZON - BARNES & NOBLE - APPLE BOOKS - KINDLE
SPOTIFY - APPLE MUSIC

C O M B O
PAPERBACK/AUDIOBOOK
ACTIVATION

Please register your book to receive the link to your audiobook version. Register at:
https://baknguyen.com/vaccine-registry

FROM THE SAME AUTHOR
Dr Bak Nguyen

www.DrBakNguyen.com

CHILDREN'S BOOK
with William Bak

The Trilogy of Legends

THE SPIES AND ALIENS COLLECTION

DENTISTRY

COVIDCONOMICS 074
THE GENERATION AHEAD
BY Dr BAK NGUYEN

THE POWER OF YES

TITLES AVAILABLE AT

www.DrBakNguyen.com

AMAZON - BARNES & NOBLE - APPLE BOOKS - KINDLE
SPOTIFY - APPLE MUSIC

DR.

Bak Nguyen